W. L. Hall

New System of Horse Training

Consists of a through Management of all the Evil Habitsknown to Horse

Flesh

W. L. Hall

New System of Horse Training
Consists of a through Management of all the Evil Habitsknown to Horse Flesh

ISBN/EAN: 9783337212179

Printed in Europe, USA, Canada, Australia, Japan

Cover: Foto ©Andreas Hilbeck / pixelio.de

More available books at **www.hansebooks.com**

NEW SYSTEM

–OF–

HORSE TRAINING

Consists of a Thorough Manage-

ment of all the

EVIL HABITS

Known to Horse Flesh

-----O-----

HE DOES WHAT HE TEACHES.

PREFACE.

In presenting this work to the public, I well understand that it will be criticised, but I have the consciousness that when the public comprehends my "New Theory" of horse breaking and training it will be appreciated. This work is especially designed to supply the need of the busy farmer and stock raiser. The author has been impressed with the almost universal lack of ability to judge accurately of the value of a horse; therefore the subject of training has received elaborate consideration, and as the value of an animal depends greatly on the care and success with which it has been trained, it is believed that the attention given to it will be productive of valuable results. The age of an animal has an important bearing in estimating both value and use. To cover this point of vital interest, I have introduced an entirely New Method and instruction as will enable any one, by a little study and observation, to ascertain with perfect accuracy the age of an animal at any period. The value of this knowledge cannot well be overestimated. With this information, and the ability to understand special characteristics and defects, the arts of the jockey will be effectually provided against.

Breaking and Training Horses.

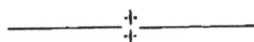

————✠————

TO CATCH A COLT OR WILD HORSE.

Turn him into a small yard, where there is no chance to run very far, or break away; it would alarm him too much to try to catch and hold him to put on the halter, and bridle, there is danger of being hurt. This difficulty you can easily overcome as follows: Take a pole, ten or twelve feet in length, or as much longer as you can use to advantage, and handle him with it, until perfectly regardless of being touched or handled with a pole, and then proceed carefully to put the halter on, by petting and caressing him. At all events, you must be careful and patient, taking time, and repeating until you are sure of success.

TO CATCH A BROKE HORSE.

Follow him, as if you did not care to catch him, and he will naturally go to the corner of the yard or pasture. He will invariably try to keep his rear parts toward you, but gently throw clods of dirt, small stones, cobs or any thing else that you can without injuring him, until he reverses his position, then walk carefully toward him, and proceed in this manner until you catch him. Just keep your temper, and you will be able to catch any horse in a short time.

TO BREAK A COLT TO LEAD.

Put a halter on him, tie a loop in his tail, pass the halter stale through the loop, keeping hold of the end of stale, drawing gently, starting him at the same time. You must move with the colt keeping yourself and him in the same position, after he has traveled for some time in this manner, change to other side and proceed as stated above. Always remember a horse must be handled on both sides, for his brain is divided. You must educate one side as well as the other.

HITCHING THE COLT SO THAT HE CAN-NOT LEARN TO PULL.

Hitch the colt a few times as follows, and he will never learn the habit. Buckle a strap around the front foot just above the hoof. Bore a hole in the manger, put the halter stale through the hole, and tie to the strap, which is buckled around his foot. The moment the colt attempts to pull, he is disconcerted and disabled, and comes ahead, from the fact of his foot being jerked from under him in surprise.

ANOTHER METHOD.

Provide yourself with a small rope, not over one-half an inch in diameter, one that cannot be broken, twenty feet long; double this, and put the end forming a loop under the tail, bring forward over the back, twisting two or three times; now pass the cords forward on each side of neck through the halter ring, and tie to the manger. If you wish to be very particular, wind the part of the rope under the tail with a piece of a rag to prevent making the tail sore. There is pressure upon the head to which he becomes accustomed; and all inclination to pulling is prevented and overcome. Another way is to make a longer loop, put the loop on like ordinary breeching, bringing it up on his back, twisting and passing the cords in the same manner as the above. When once broken, however, they are honest and reliable afterwards.

PRELIMINARY BITTING.

My advice is to bit your colts when two years

old preparing them for actual bitting and training. You cannot handle a colt too much, the more the better. First thing in bitting a colt, take a piece of three-eights inch rope about four feet long; put rope into colt's mouth, the some as a bit, and bring up and tie on top of head, let him loose to run around the yard until he gets used to bit. Then take the same rope, place in mouth just as before, bring rope back af far as collar goes, tie on top of neck tight enough so that it will stay in colt's mouth, then gradually tighten until you get his head in the position you wish him to carry it.

BOSS BITTING AND BREAKING RIG.

The boss bitting and breaking rig is the best on earth. Why is this called the "Boss Bitting and Breaking Rig?" Because it is the conqueror of colts and horses, no matter how ugly or vicious they are, this rig will beat them out every time. It will conquer the kicker, sulker, runaway and etc. The boss bitting rig consists of two pieces of rope, each fifty-five feet in length of three-eights and five-eights inch rope. The three-eights rope is used for bridle, bridle-reins, check-reins, side check-reins, martingales and driving lines. The five-eights is for harness. The first step is to take five-eights rope, double this, tie a knot about four feet from the centre using the loop for breeching letting it come lower than ordinary breeching, placing the knot just in front of hips in centre of back, slip knot on rope so as to adjust it properly, to bring breeching to fit the horse you are breaking. Tie another knot so it will come on top of his neck just where the collar goes. Bring the ends of rope, one on each side of neck, like a collar, cross in front and pass back in place of tug or side strap to breeching, putting the rope through the breeching at the flank, passing the rope under the belly to opposite sides, putting once around tug rope at the place, where the tug buckle is on common harness, bringing it up to back rope, putting each rope over single back rope, then down around tug rope back of belly rope carrying forward putting around the collar rope and tug rope, back to where tug and back rope comes together which forms the big buckle, leaving ends of rope hanging. The purpose for which they are used will be shown farther on. To completo our "Boss Bitting Rig" we must have a bridle. Take three-eights rope, double it, tie a knot in centre forming a loop to put in the mouth, like bits, having the knot come on the nose, where the nose piece of halter comes, tie another knot about eight or ten inches above the first knot, so that it will come at the roots of fore-top, putting fore-top through knot, bringing the ropes between the ears tying a loop in each piece of rope at base of ear for gag runners, passing the ropes down on each side of the head, crossing under the jaw to opposite side, putting through the loop which is in the mouth, take a string and tie the ropes together, where they cross under the jaw, and from there put them through the gag runners, passing back through back rope of harness, bringing forward through bridle bit or loop in the the mouth, draw the rope and tie if, so that it will bear on him to suit yourself, pass the remaining rope between fore legs, and fasten to belly rope for martingales. This makes you the best and cheapest bitting, that can be made. Care must be taken not to bring too much restraint up on the bit by tying the ropes too short, at first. It is bad policy to keep a colt checked up too long at a time, as it becomes tiresome, which would cause the disagreeable habit of sulking. If, however the colt should fight the restraint of the bit or check, it should be left on till the fit exhausts itself, and he shows a disposition to submit to its restraint. Short lessons at first, and gradually keeping on longer as the mouth becomes hardened by the bit and the colt will bear it without fatigue, is the best course. When thoroughly bitted in this manner, he will also be broke to harness. You are now ready for the next step of teaching, to-rein right and left, stop, start back, etc. Untie rope used for check-reins, side-reins and martingales to use for lines. Bring lines back on each side of the colt, passing off line around the hind-legs just above hock-joints, you standing on near side of him about four feet from flank, with a line in each hand, pull on the near line, starting the colt at the same time. You are leading as well as driving him. Work the colt easily till he leans what you want him to do, then reverse position. Always remember to keep on the side of the colt, with one line around the hock, until he drives well. A colt can buck, kick and jump as much as he wishes to, but as long as you keep this position you will have full control of him. If the colt should, in some way, get the start of you, drop one of the lines, stand still, and let him run and jump until willing to stop. If he is just cunning and treacherous enough to be watching for advantage, and you are afraid you cannont keep control of him, put the tripper on, and use it well. You can soon bring him to time. After your colt is well broken in this manner, take two poles, nine and one-half feet long, bore a hole one and one-half feet from the end, in both poles, put ends of rope mentioned before, hanging to harness, through the holes in the poles bringing this end of them up in position of thills, tying in place, then tie the other ends together with a rope three and a half feet a part. Drive him around in the poles until there is perfect submission to them, guiding promptly to the reins, and submitting to the poles striking the flank or heels without exciting the least fear. Just as soon as he reins well, you are all right.

TO TEACH COLT TO BACK.

Place your thumb nail on a nerve on the inside of the point of the shoulder, each side of the breast, and say "back." Then pet him and he will soon learn to back at the word.

TO BREAK COLTS TO DRIVE SINGLE.

After driving your colt in poles as described before, put on your harness, in most cases it is perfectly safe to hitch them into road cart or sulky. I advise putting on my popular tripper when hitched up for the first time, so if he should become frightened you can check him at once. A few lessons of this type will bring him out straight.

DRIVING DOUBLE.

The first point, I would call your especial attention is the fittimg of the harness; it should in every respect fit well, and should not be drawn to tight anywhere. See that the bridle fits well, that the cheek pieces are long enough to let the bit rest naturally and easily in the mouth; always using a good solid harness; also seeing that your whiffletree and neck-yoke are safe. When first hitching colt or colts up let your vehicle be the front part of a bob-sled, driving until they are thoroughly broken to drive double; always remembering not to worry the colt, as it irritates and raises his temper. Do not drive him when hungry or thirsty. Next put your colt on to a lumber wagon, driving him slow at first. Do not make the draught heavy, as he cannot be expected to draw like an old horse without experience and practice. The great trouble with most people, in training colts, is, they attempt too much; and doing too much now is liable to spoil all. Loud "yelling" or cracking of the whip should not be permitted under any circumstances.

THE TRIPPER OR W.

The tripper is used to subdue a horse of any bad habits; such as the following: running-away, kicking, rearing, etc. This is important to all horse owners and raisers. To make the tripper, provide yourself with a piece of rope, eight feet long; tie three rings in the rope about one foot apart; put the rope around the horse just back of fore legs, like a saddle girt, letting centre ring come under centre of the belly; then put a strap with a ring on, around each fore foot. Take a rope, twenty feet in length, run one end through the ring on near side of the horse, then through the ring on the near foot, putting back through the centre ring then through the ring on the other foot, bringing up to ring on off side of horse and tie securely. Take hold of the other end of the rope, and stand back of the horse. When he rears and pitches jerk his feet from under him, letting him down gently until he is willing to give up. This is a valuable means of control; it enables carrying out in the easiest and most practical manner, with perfect safety. It is especially valuable on a doubtful, reckless, runaway horse. With this "Tripper" you have the most powerful horse helpless, without injury to him. If the ground is hard or frozen, put pads on the knees for fear of injuring them.

GAG STRAP.

Take a heavy leather strap, four feet nine inches in length, one inch and one quarter in width, with buckle on one end, make a roll in centre of strap, ten inches in length, or in other words make it like crupper. When the gag strap is finished the gag should be three inches in circumference. This gag strap is a wonderful horse tamer of itself. It subdues, it drives, it melts, it coaxes, and it conquers. If you do not believe it try it on "Satin." Try this on your kicky cows and it will work like a charm.

TO LEAD A VICIOUS HORSE WITH A HALTER.

To lead a vicious horse is a dangerous act. Horse owners generally shrink from but it is made easy by using my halter-hitch. Have your halter fit well, standing on near side of the horse, bring your halter strap over his nose in same position as nose-piece, holding the halter stale with right hand in place, take hold of stale at nose-piece with left hand putting over nose-piece and into his mouth. This gives you a purchase on the upper-jaw and at the same time it effects the nerve, and goes to the brain of the horse. My ''halter-hitch'' is a horse cooler.

WHY THE HORSE REQUIRES INTELLI-GENT MANAGEMENT.

It is because horses are intelligent animals. They have a sense of reason, which may be improved by training. They are naturally disposed to rely upon their masters, and this disposition should never be overcome by the fear of injury. They are courageous, and at the same time timid. Their courage should be fosterd, since it increases their spirit and decreases their timidity.

They fear objects with which they are unfamiliar. Once they learn that an object is harmless they cease to fear it. Thus they may be accustomed to the sound and sight of a locomotive, one of the most fearful objects to them naturally, and if allowed to satisfy themselves that a locomotive is not dangerous, they will at length want to touch it with the nose; for this is the last means a horse uses to fully satisfy himself that an object will not injure him. Thus satisfied, all further fear of that object is passed.

SULKY COLTS.

There is another type of extreme, usually colts, I frequently find, which are apparently very bad, and which I hate above almost any other horse. A great many colts will show sulks as soon as you get the halter on. This class of colts should be handled with great care to prevent them from getting sulky. When you commence breaking, it takes a great deal of patience and time to successfuly break them, but when well broken they make the best horses. I find the best way to treat a sulky colt is to be kind with him at first, and if that does not succeed, then to use harsher means until he throws himself as he is sure to do. As soon as he is down, get two quarts of clear, clean water, keep him down, hold up his head and pour the water into his nose. This smothers him so he will at once get on to his feet. They will not throw themselves but a few times. I have broken the very worst sulkers in this way.

BALKING IN DOUBLE HARNESS.

This is to the horse man a most perplexing and difficult horse to manage. There is no chance to get at him to make him work. The whip is the usual remedy, which will only make matters worse; yet nothing is easier to do than to make this class of horses come to terms. There are a great many remedies for starting balky horses, but what I propose to do is to teach you how to break a balky horse successfully. If you have a genuine balky horse, take him at once and put the tripper on, handle him with it until you get him to understand that you are his master, and he entirely gives up. A great many men give up before the horse does. When the horse is perfectly subdued you can handle him with ease. After handling in this manner, put the harness on. Be sure the collar fits well. You must make him understand that you are his friend as long as he obeys the word of command. Then hitch him to a small pole, starting him to right or left drawing the pole, when he has drawn the pole from right to left for some time, stop and pet him to let him know he has done right, never pet him only when he obeys. Increase your load a little at a time until he will pull every time you speak to him. I would suggest hitching him to a stone boat if you cannot get a pole. If at any time the horse should try to play his old tricks, apply the tripper at once rather harshly. In this manner I can break any balky horse that you bring me. I will give you some more remedies for starting balky horses.

REMEDY NUMBER ONE.

Put the gag strap on the horse, in nine cases out of ten this will be sufficient without using my "Popular Tripper".

REMEDY NUMBER TWO.

Put a pully on end of the wagon tongue, buckle a strap around each fore-leg above the knee, tie a rope in the strap on the off leg then pass through pully on end of the tongue, and tie in strap on near leg. Start your true horse and the balky horse will have to move.

RUNAWAY BRIDLE.

The following very simple form of overdraw will be found very valuable, because so simple and easily made, if you have a good piece of cord, or any small but strong cord, you can make a rig in a few minutes, that enables you to drive a bad horse with perfect ease. First, take a cord, eighteen or twenty feet in length. Put the centre of cord on top of the head under the bridle, about ten inches from this centre, tie loop knot making check or gag runner which will come up near the ears. Pass each end down and through the mouth, then up and through the loops before named, then back through the turrets to the wagon, same as reins. The higher the gag-runners, the more purchase up and back. Wherever I have introduced my runaway bridle, it is considered very valuable.

RUNAWAY HORSE.

Put on Boss Bitting Rig harness, all complete, leaving lines ready for driving, put him between

two poles as described for breaking colts; also put
on the tripper, handle him in this manner until
he is thoroughly subdued. Then hitch him to a
wagon, with the tripper on, so he will not get
the advantage of you in case he should try his
old tricks. Should he undertake to run give
him the full benefit of the "Tripper", at the same
time speak to him the word of command; Whoa!
A few lessons of this kind will break any horse of
this habit.

SAFETY BIT.

For bit take a square piece of three-eights
iron, with a hole in each end, making guards to
bit eight inches in length, put these guards
through the holes in the bit, so that they will
work easily, then make a loop on each end of
guard, buckle checks of bridle into gaurds of bit,
drawing guards about two thirds through bit,
buckle lines into lower end of guards. You have
a bit that will hold any horse.

KICKING IN THE HARNESS.

Horse men find this habit to be the most
perplexing and dangerous a horse can have. It

is not every man that is capable of managing a kicking horse. It has taken many hours of study and practice to successfully break and. overcome the very bad cases of kicking horses. I have tried many things in vain, but I finally succeeded in accomplishing the object which I have been in search of. I feel rewarded for all the time I have spent in obtaining the knowledge. I expect while importing this knowledge to others to feel that I have benefited the world, as well as my self, and save a great many useless horses to do good work for their master safely, it is well understood among horse owners that a kicking horse is not very valuable and certainly not safe, for any use unless redeemed from the habit. I am glad to know that there is a "Balm in Gilead" for the kicker. It is very seldom that you find geldings that are addicted to kicking, but you frequently find mares that kick. That is not the only habit they have either while kicking. The kicking is always accompanied by the switching of the tail and throwing the urine. I have found that you can not successfully break a horse of kicking until you have succeeded in breaking him of switching the tail. The first step in breaking a horse of switching the tail is to put

on a harness leaving off the crupper and back
strap, take a strap and tie your collar down to
the belly band, so the collar can not raise and
choke him, next divide the hair on his tail equal,
tying a loop in each divide, then take two ropes,
six feet in length, tie one in each loop of the
tail, turn tail up over the back of the horse drawing the other end of each rope through the lower
hame rings, draw these ropes rather tight being
careful to have the tail drawn exactly straight
over the centre of the back, leaving in this position for thirty minutes. In most cases this will
break a horse of switching the tail, for it stretches
the cords in the side of the tail, preventing them
of rolling the tail, as all kickers have a peculiar
roll to the tail before kicking. It does not prevent them from using the tail otherwise. Should
one trial not be sufficient give them another dose.
You now have your horse broken of switching
the tail. I consider the task more than half
done. The next step is to always put on a blind
bridle, take a rope, double, and tie into the rings
of the bit useing rope for lines the same as for
breaking colts, put on the tripper, and hitch him
between two, poles. Drive him with tripper
on until he is convinced that to kick is a very

great hardship, this they soon learn by experience. Every time he tries to kick, take his feet from under him. He will soon learn that the old adage, "Try, try again", is not true in his case. After you have given him this lesson, put him in the barn until morning. For fear of accident proceed as before, but it is a very few horses that I have had to put the tripper on the third time. Now take off the tripper and hitch on to a wagon with a good steady horse, and be careful for the first few times not to irritate him. The first time you hitch him up after you take the tripper off, put on a set of breeching letting the breeching down low, running the side straps to the bit, having them loose enough so he can travel without jerking his mouth. If he should attempt to kick with this rig on, the punishment would be so great, it would check him and a few trials will surely break him. In every case be sure and show your friendship, as soon as he becomes docile.

CARRYING HORSE'S TAIL TO ONE SIDE.

This is usually a deformity, or a contraction of one of the cords of the tail. In many cases it detracts from the value of the animal as it spoils them for a fine carriage horse. This deformity is a contraction that cannot be overcome readily as it usually takes about two weeks to successfully perform the operation. Put collar and hames on the horse leaving the crupper off, tie a rope into tail and draw it to the opposite side from which he carries it, fasten rope to hame ring and draw it very tight, leave him in this condition for thirty minutes, if this should not be sufficient give him another dose of one hour, it may take several days to accomplish the desired end. You will have to be patient and let time do its work. Should you draw it to much, change it to the other side and proceed in this manner until the cure is affected.

HARD BITTED HORSES.

Winding the bit with woolen yarn will prevent most horses from pulling on the bit. Another method, which never fails, is to make a small leather roll about the size of a common lead pencil, fasten the ends together firmly and loop it on a common straight bit in the centre, pass the loop over the upper jaw and under the lip. You can hold your horse with one hand with your bit fixed this way.

TO BREAK A HORSE OF BITING.

On going in to a stall with a biting horse, take a sharp peg in your hand, when he attempts to bite you, jab him in the nose with the peg, he will soon turn his head from you. Take a piece of hard wood, six inches in length. make it three cornerd, cut the edges as sharp as possible, have it just thick enough, so that when it is in his mouth he can not shut his teeth together, place the stick in his mouth tie a string to one end and pass it over his head and tie to other end. You will notice that there are no teeth where the stick comes. If he will not now attempt to bite you when you approach him, bother him and get him mad and he will soon try to bite you, but instead of biting you he will bite the stick and punish himself.

TO PREVENT HORSES ROLLING IN STALL.

Take a rope, the length from ceiling to floor less the length of horse's head and one inch more, fasten one end to the ceiling, the other to the halter on top of his head. It is impossible for a horse to roll, when he cannot reach the floor with his nose.

REMEDY NO. 2.

Take a surcingle, fasten a temporary pad to it, made with brad nails in, so that when he undertakes to roll, the nails will prick him.

TO BREAK HORSE OF PAWING IN STABLE.

Buckle a strap around the fore leg above the knee, put on a piece of chain, eight or ten inches long, so that when he paws the chain will strike his leg.

REMEDY NO. 2.

Put a surcingle around horse's body, and then buckle a strap around surcingle and his fore leg, so that every time he tries to paw it will check him.

KICKING WITH ONE FOOT IN THE STABLE.

A great many nervous horses form a habit of kicking with one foot in the stable while eating, caused by being irritated by another horse. To break them, buckle a strap with a piece of chain, eight or ten inches long, around his leg above the hock, so the chain will hit his leg every time he kicks. Self punishment will break any horse.

TO BREAK HORSE KICKING WITH BOTH FEET IN BARN.

Place a piece of plank across the stall, over the hips, about an inch higher than the horse's hips. At each effort to kick his hips now strike the plank and will prevent his kicking.

TO BREAK HORSE OF KICKING AT A PERSON IN STABLE.

Put on gag-strap, then you can put on the tripper with perfect safety, when you get the tripper on take the gag-strap off, and proceed to handle him, do not be too lenient with him at first. At the first signs of kicking give him the full benefit of the tripper, and he will shortly understand that kicking does not pay. A few lessons of this kind will cure him.

TONGUE HANGING OUT OF THE MOUTH.

Some horses have the habit of carrying the tongue out of the mouth at one side. This habit is generally confined to a narrow jawed horses. The space between the molar teeth being too narrow to contain the tongue in the mouth when bit presses upon it, many times the teeth becomes rough and have sharp edges which irritate the tougue, and causes the horse to put his tongue over the bit and hang it out one side of the mouth. To break this habit, examine the teeth, if you find the edges of the teeth sharp and rough have them floated smooth, should the cause be not in the teeth, if it is only a habit, take a bit and drill two holes through it, put copper wire in to holes so as to form two bows in the mouth between the teeth, making the size of bow four inches in length when finished.

ANOTHER REMEDY.

Use a straight bit and get a strong piece of elastic rubber to put around the bit and horse's tongue. I find the following way to be very good. Fasten the bit in the upper part of his mouth by tying the bit to nose piece of halter.

TO BREAK A HORSE OF STRIKING.

First put on a gag strap, after having gag on, put on Tripper, handle him until he will let you go around him without offering to strike you. A few lessons of this kind will break him entirely.

TO PREVENT HORSES FROM STRIKING.

Put on breeching and collar, put the rope back through breeching at flank, the same as for breaking colts, let ropes come from breeching to forelegs, and fasten above the knees. You have your horse so you can work around his fore parts with out fear of injury.

JUMPING HORSES.

Punch a hole in each ear, when you turn him out tie them together. He will not jump unless he can work his ears. Another plan is to put on each foot of a horse a strap with a ring on it, put a surcingle around him with two rings on it, one ring on each side, take a strong cord or rope, fasten one end to the ring on the hind foot, then pass it up through the ring in the surcingle, down to the ring on the fore foot. Leave the cords, of the right length to allow the horse to stand naturally, and not to hinder him from travelling. Fix a horse in this manner and he can not jump.

TO DRENCH A HORSE.

Take a small stout cord, tie it around the neck, then pass it under the upper lip, over his head, down under his lip, through the cord around his neck. With this cord you can doctor your horse without the assistance of anyone.

THE AGE OF A HORSE.

Every owner of horses has a way of his own of judging of a horse's age. This is something that puzzles men more than any one thing about a horse, as a great many horse dealers cut off and tamper with horse's teeth. It is getting popular with the trading fraternity to change the teeth, so that an inexperienced party cannot tell an old horse from a young horse. I have made it a study to correct some of the old theories now extant. My theory of testing a horse's age, I think when understood will be found to be the easiest and most accurate method of telling the age of a horse, as I do not depend on one method alone. There are variations to all known rules, the difference being in the way horses are fed, therefore I give two complete methods. By comparing the two methods you never can be deceived in the age of a horse. The colt when two years old looses his two centre nippers or front teeth, when three years old he looses the next two nippers, when four years old the corner nippers, when five years old he has a full mouth, when six years old the corner nippers are full size and are more level, when seven years old the cups or grooves in the two centre nippers disappear, when eight the cups in the adjoining nippers disappear, when nine the cups in the corner nippers disappear. Nine men out of ten in examining the teeth of the horse to ascertain the age, examine the upper jaw. The lower jaw should be examined also; as the teeth of the lower jaw show wear and change their appearance more surely than the upper jaw. Hence both jaws should be examined. When ten years old a groove or mark appears just beneath the gum on the corner nipper on the upper jaw, when twenty one years old this groove will be at the bottom of the tooth. It takes eleven years for the tooth to ware up to the groove or mark. You judge of the age of the horse by the distance of the mark down on the tooth. For instance, to illustrate; if the mark on the tooth was half way down, the horse would be between fifteen and sixteen years of age. It is generally supposed by many people that horse's teeth are continually growing, but this is a mistake. A horse's teeth does not grow after he is fully developed. The gums gradually shrinks away and leave more of the tooth exposed to view. On the other hand the teeth are gradually wearing away instead of growing. A satisfactory proof of this is did you ever see an old horse have the lampers?

METHOD NUMBER TWO.

Every five years of a horse's life the ribs separate, or in other words the muscle shrinks away and leaves a space that can easily be felt commencing with the rear ribs, when ten years old you will readily perceive that the next two ribs are parted. Every five years thereafter a rib will part or separate as long as the horse lives. If you are careful to apply both methods you will not buy many twenty year old horses for nine year old.

THE TEETH.

I am coming to a subject now that is the most neglected of any about a horse. A great many people think if they feed and clean a horse that is all that is necessary or if sometimes the horse is taken violently sick with bots, belly ache or some other disease, there must be something done immediately, or the horse will die. In my

experience I have found that farmers feed a great
many bushels of grain more than they would need
to feed if they took more pains to understand
that important subject, the teeth. If a horse
commences to run down the cause given is hard
work or something else, never thinking that the
horse has an ulcerated tooth and is at the very
time groaning, or would groan if he could make
his master understand what was the matter of
him. I was once called to see an ugly horse, the
owner said that the horse had always been very
kind but in the last few days he would not allow
any one to touch him, and was getting vicious,
would not eat but stand all day with his head
down acting as if he was in pain, he also said that
every thing had been don : that he could think
of, but nothing had seem :d to alleviate him, now
the fact was, that no one had even thought the
horse had teeth, that cou!.d ache or ulcerate. I
made the remark to the owner that it might be
possible that the horse had an ulcerated tooth,
oh how he laughed, Ha! Ha! It only took a
few minutes to convince him I was right. I took
my mouth opener and stepped upto the horse,
put it in his mouth and showed him the ulcerated
tooth. He said "is that possible!" "I have

owned horses for twenty years and had never thought of a horse having such a thing as that." I took my forceps and pulled the tooth and in less than ten minutes the horse was eating. It would astonish horse owners, if all the facts were known about horses teeth. How many horses die on the account of their teeth every year. A great many think that when old horses do not grind their food properly, the cause is old age, and the front teeth being to long not letting the back teeth come together, this is erroneous, as the front teeth are no longer at twenty years old than at seven years old. If a horse commences to run down in flesh it is most always thought that his digestion is bad and the owner will start for the drug store for condition powders, when the facts are the horse is suffering from his teeth, and in my teaching I try to impress up on the minds of men this important subject for I consider it of so much importance, that I have made it a special plea in my book for the benefit of the noble horse. One thing I wish to bring before your minds especially is the fact that like men, horses lose their teeth, and when a horse loses a tooth the one opposite does not wear off and therefore it becomes long enough so that it will come in contact with the gum and will at each move of the horse's jaw cut into the gum and hurt him, so that he will swallow quite a large amount of food without grinding it properly. You will see that he does not get the full benefit of the food you give him. A great many times a horse's teeth do not wear alike, leaving corners on the teeth that are not worn down, these corners or edges with every movement of the jaw will come in contact with the cheek, and cause an irritation and soreness, when this is the case, the horse while eating hard grain will turn his head to one side, just as if he was going to throw it out, and will show a great deal of uneasiness while eating. This can easily be remedied by any veterinary.

TO SHOE A VICIOUS HORSE.

Put on the gag strap. If this should fail, take a common rum or tie strap, put a slip noose around the horse's leg just above the gambrel or hock joint, pull on the strap. He will soon give up his foot, keep the strap tight. You can shoe him with ease. Another method. Tie a knot in horse's tail, buckle a strap in loop of tail with a ring on it, then buckle a strap with a ring on it, on his ankle, tie a rope into the ring in the tail, run the rope through the ring on the ankle, back through the ring on the tail, pull on the rope, bringing foot in position for shoeing. To shoe in front. Put a surcingle around the horse attach a rope to foot, draw his foot up and hold it until he will give up. To clinch, have the collar on and put the rope through it.

TO BREAK A HORSE OF SCARING AT BUFFALO, UMBRELLA ETC.

Put the halter-hitch on your horse, holding him firmly by the halter stale, moving the article toward him carefully in this manner, until you can get him to smell or feel of it with his nose. A horse's sense of feeling is located in the nose.

ANOTHER METHOD.

Put on the tripper, and handle him as described above. If occasion requires, take his feet from under him, while in this condition approach him with the article, which he is afraid of. Always remember that kindness is the first law of nature.

ESTABLISHED IN 1866.

————o————

A. D. CLARKE & CO.,

ALGONA, KOSSUTH CO., IOWA,

————o————

Have Good Stock, Grazing And
Farming Lands For Sale at
From $6.50 to $12.50 Per Acre.

————o————

EASY PAYMENTS AND
LONG TIME.

————o————

These are The Only Low Priced
LANDS LEFT IN IOWA.

CORNS.

They are the result of uneven pressure of the shoe, too much bearing on the quarters. Remove the shoe, cut out the bruised part, fill with equal parts of turpentine and lard, sear with a hot iron. REMEDY NO. 2.—Fill the cavity with brown sugar, burn the sugar in with a hot iron.

ACUTE FOUNDER.

Sometimes it is caused by overwork, in which the feet are pounded and sored up, drinking cold water when warm, or standing in draught when heated will cause it. What to do, give one quart of raw linseed oil at a dose. Pull off the shoes, and pare the shell of the feet down, so as to let him stand on the sole of the foot. Rub the forelegs well with water as hot as it can be borne without scalding. It is also a good plan to start the blood in each foot at the point of the frog. Give two ounces of pulverized alum every two hours, for twelve hours, and then three times a day until he is better, keep bowels loose.

ANOTHER RECEIPT.

MIX.—One ounce sweet spirits of nitre,
One dram tincture of aconite root,
One ounce potash nitrate,
One-half pt. of water.

For a dose, give a table-spoonful every two hours, until the fever abates, and the patient becomes comfortable, then give three times a day.

PRICKING FROM NAILS.

Pricking may come from a nail running into the quick when shoeing, or a nail may be picked up in the street.

REMEDY.—When you have removed the shoe, and found where the prick is, pare out the hole, and around it a little, to thin the hoof; this will relieve the pressure, when it begins to swell, turn in a small quantity of solution of carbolic acid, one part of acid to twenty of water, or use a little turpentine.

CALKS.

Calks are cuts and bruises on the caronet, or soft parts above it, caused by one foot stepping upon the other, and the calk of the shoe if sharp, cuts in to the flesh. It is most common in fall, winter and spring, when mud and snow are deep. What to do.—MIX.—One-half ounce carbolic acid, in one pint of water.

THRUSH.

Thrush is the name given to a disease of the frog. It is a rotting or ulceration of the frog, and is attended with a very offensive, black, watery discharge. The frog rots completly off sometimes, and extends down in the cleft between the heels, to a depth of from half an inch to two inches. What to do.—Trim off all the ragged parts of the frog, clear out all the holes and crevices with a case knife, or with some similar instrument, then apply a linseed poultice, with charcoal powdered over the surface. After twenty-four hours, clear it all off, and dress the effected parts with calomel, well introduced into all the cracks, with a case knife. Repeat this once or twice, letting a day intervene between the applications. When it is all dried up, dress the part with pine tar.

Prevention.—Pick out the feet well, each day, to let the air in around the frog, which is necessary to keep them healthy.

BONE SPAVIN.

A bone spavin is an enlargement of the lower part of the hock joint. At the first appearance of the bone spavin there will be a lameness, more or less acute according to the amount of injury to the joint. The lameness will be distinguished by a stiffness in moving from side to side in the stall, after the horse has been driven a short time and gets warmed up, he will go all right, until he is allowed to cool off, when he start off worse then ever, until warmed up again. The cause of this is, by standing, the joint becomes dry, and great pain attends the flexion of it, but the exercise excites the secretion of joint oil, which lubricates it, and the horse is comfortable till the joint gets dry again.

REMEDY.—Two ounces of turpentine, bathe the parts freely, putting on four layers of flannel and applying a hot flat-iron thoroughly heating in. Repeat until cured. The horse should not be heavy worked while under treatment.

BOG SPAVIN.

How to know it. - There will be a large soft swelling on the inner and front aspect of the hock. The swelling is of the same character as wind galls; it seems to be filled with air, but it is synovia. What to do.—Bathe it as continuously as possible with either hot or cold water for twelve hours, then apply an oil-meal poultice, hot and soft. Continue the poultice for several days. changing it for one day, and bathing with hot water at the time of changing. When the soreness and lameness are gone apply the following liniment twice a day.

MIX.—Three ounces tincture of iodine,
One ounce aqua ammonia,
One ounce turpentine,
One ounce of glycerine.

CURB.

The curb is an enlargement on the back of the hock and a little below it. What to do.—In a recent case, when the sprained tendons and the ligaments are sore, swollen and hot, bathe the part with water, three or four times aday, for a half hour at a time. Raise the heel an inch, continue this treatment till all soreness is gone. Then apply turpentine to the affected part and rub downward with a smooth round piece of wood, and give three or four weeks of rest.

RING-BONE.

Is an enlargement of the pastern joint. What to do.—Apply turpentine and hot flat the same as for bone spavin.

SPLINT.

A splint is an enlargement on the cannon bone just below the knee usually on the inside, but it is some times on the out side. What to do.—If noticed when the injury first occurs, apply either hot or cold water with the cooling lotion,

MIX.—One ounce muriate of ammonia,
One ounce salt petre,
One quart of water.

Till the soreness is nearly gone, then apply blister made as follows:

MIX.—One half ounce powdered cantharides,
Two drams red iodid of mercury,
Four ounces of lard.

Give a couple weeks of rest.

SWEENEY.

How to know it. The shoulder and leg are carried forward all a piece: no knee action: the shoulder carried forward and the leg sweeney: at the time the leg is being taken forward the head is nodded down at the start and suddenly jerked up, toward the finish of the action. There is an inability to raise the leg to step over an obstacle a foot high, but he will drag the leg over. Swelling, heat and soreness are noticed. If allowed to run on with out treatment, will keep getting worse, when lameness is localed in shoulder, use the following preparation. When the sprains as sweeney first appears bathe well with the following liniment.

    MIX.—2 oz. organum oil,
          2 oz. oil spike,
          2 oz. oil cedar,
          1 pt alcohol,

Apply to shoulder or affected parts also good for a sprain of any kind. If the above should not effect a cure then put in what is called a blind rowel to fill out the shrinkage cut a small hole at the upper part of the shoulder just large enough to admit your finger, put your finger inside of hole and work the hide and tendons loose from the bone all around the hole, then cut a piece of leather round and about three inches in diameter with a small hole in center, double it and put it in to hole and smooth out smooth, and put a piece of poke root in hole cut in leather, this starts an iritation and starts it to running it will work to the bottom of shoulder and the shoulder will fill out so you never would know it had been sweened, the leather works as far down as there is any disease and after it gets to bottom of shoulder take it out. I have seen horses sweened bad that had never limped a step nor shown any signs of lameness, and the shoulder had shrunk away badly.

HOW TO LOCATE A HORSE'S LAMENESS.

Lead your horse over a pole or wagon tongue, about a foot high. If the lameness is in the shoulder he will always put the well foot over the pole first, if he comes up so it would come right for him to put the lame leg over first he will stop and put the well foot over first. If lameness is below the shoulder, he will put one foot over the pole as quick as the other.

SCRATCHES OR CRACKED HEEL.

Scratched or cracked heels are simply chaps and cracks around the heels, and in the hallow of the pastern, they correspond to chapped hands in man. What to do.—When the horse comes in, wipe off the parts as nicely as possible, bandage them with a flannel to keep them warm and when dry clean them thoroughly with a brush not touching them with water at all. Thorough-cleanse the blood, by giving saltpetre, sulpher, copperas of equal parts. Pulverize fine, give two tablespoonfuls per day. Then apply an ointment made of lard and pounded alum in equal parts.

ANOTHER REMEDY. —Apply human dung to afflicted parts once a day for three days, and then wash with soft water and castile soap. Always wipe dry. Repeat until cured.

HEAVES.

It is incureable, but 'it can be alleviated by careful feeding and so controlled that only the best judge of a horse will notice it. Wet every thing he eats, and give the following mixture twice a day in soft feed for a week and then once a week.

MIX.—Two ounces powdered lobelia seed,
Two ounces linseed meal.

Never check up a heavey horse.

STOCKING.

Stocking is the name given to swelling of the legs, usually confined to the parts below the knees and hocks, although in bad cases it extends above these joints. Causes.—Weakness of the tissues of the legs, being unable to support the pressure above; weak, watery, impoverished condition of the blood, and the legs being the most dependent part it settles on them. · Standing still is a very common cause so much so that there is a good deal of it just from standing from night till morning. It is most common in badly drained and illy ventilated stables. Young horses are more subject to it than older ones. It is often a symptom of some disease that requires attention; for stocking in disease is always a symptom of weakness which needs tonics and stimulants. What to do.—Give the following tonic, one powder night and morning, in the feed:

MIX.—One and one-half ounce pure sulfate of iron,
Two ounces nitrate of potash,
Powder, and divide into twelve powders.

Shower the legs with cold water in hot weather but omit the water in cold weather, give gentle exercise to reduce the swelling, and when coming in from exercise or work, bandage them tight; if in summer, use cotton bandages; in winter use flannel. Avoid all strong, irritating or blistering applications. If necessary, repeat the powders. Remove the bandages on going out for exercise, and give the legs hand-rubbing.

STIFLED HORSE.

In case of dislocation tie a rope to the pastern and pull it forward, and a little outward at the same time, the man handling the rope standing about a yard from the horse's shoulder; and another man standing at the stifle shoves the bone back in to its place, by pushing toward the horse's flank, it will slip in with a snap. Then put on a high-heeled shoe, the heels raised two inches, and bathe the stifle as continously as possible with the following:

MIX.—Ounce muriate of ammonia,
One ounce of salt petre,
One quart of water.

When the inflamation that follows is gone, apply a blister all around the joint and use the following for blister:

MIX. —One half ounce powder cantharides,
Two ounces of lard.

Give a long rest, if this does not cure in four or five weeks, a seaton may be put in over the joint running up and down about four inches; wash it clean, once or twice a day with hot water, leave it in from two to four weeks.

SPASMODIC COLIC.

How to know it.—The horse will begin to

show uneasiness and look around; raises up his hind feet toward his belly; he lies down and gets up again after lying perhaps a couple of minutes. He rolls, kicks; sweats profusely, has a haggard countenance, is inclined to turn upon his back and remain so.

REMEDY.—Mix.—Two ounces of whiskey,
One ounce extract of ginger,
Half pint of water.

Or the following: One and one-half ounces of Sweet Spirits of Nitre, one ounce of Laudunum, one-half ounce Extract of Ginger.

Always when possible give warm water injections with a very little soap in it, just to make it a little slippery.

COMMON CURE FOR COLIC.—One table-spoonful of salaratus in one pint of warm tea, or warm water if tea cannot be had. If first dose does not relieve, repeat and increase dose.

WHAT TO DO FOR WORMS.

There are numerous useful vermifuges, the most convenient of which is the following: One drachm sulphate of iron, one drachm tartar emetic, two drachms linseed meal. Mix. Give at one dose repeating it morning and evening for a week. Then give a purgative of oil and turpentine as follows: Mix, one ounce spirits of turpentine, one pint raw linseed oil. Give at one dose.

After three weeks repeat the entire treatment to catch the young worms previously left in the bowels in the form of nits or eggs, and which have hatched since.

ANOTHER.—One tea-spoonful of alum in each feed for six feeds.

LICE ON HORSES AND CATTLE.

Tobacco, two pounds, water, two gallons. Steep and wash the animal.

REMEDY NO. 2.—Carbolic acid, one tablespoonful to one quart of soft water. Apply with a brush.

CHRONIC COUGH.

REMEDY.—Two ounces liquor ammonia, two ounces spirits of turpentine, two ounces linseed oil. Apply this to the throat, well rubbing it in all around and up toward the ears. Give internally the following powders: One and one-half ounces camphor gum, one ounce digitalis, two ounces linseed meal. Powder and mix. Divide into twelve powders and give one night and morning in soft feed.

CURE FOR DISTEMPER.

Make a poultice by boiling turnips, the same as for table use, when nearly cooked stir in bran while cooking, until you have a thick poultice. After having bran and turnips thoroughly cooked stir in tobacco enough to make poultice smell strong of tobacco. Apply to throat and swollen parts. This will relieve in a few moments. Also burn some old leather by putting leather on a vessel filled with coals and holding under horse's nose so he will inhale smoke. When watering, only give a pail of water at a time with two table-spoonfuls of tincture of bromide of potassium. I have cured colts with this remedy that had been given up to die.

SURE CURE FOR SCOURS.

Fill a small cotton sack with flour and put into a kettle of water, boil until hard. Then pulverize and give to the animal until relieved.

SURE CURE FOR POLE-EVIL OR FISTULA

These diseases are both of the same nature but have different locations. The pole-evil is located on the top of the head and the fistula on the shoulders.

REMEDY.—Take a small piece of blue vitriol

that will just fit into the pipe or tube, press it down to bottom of pipe with a small stick. Be sure not to take the pipe out until it is loose at the bottom, so you can get it all. How to know when you have it all out—at the base of the pipe there is a solid piece like the end of your finger. When pipe is out keep clean by washing well each morning with soap-suds until healed.

TO CURE A NAVEL BREACH ON A COLT.

First see that all the intestines are put back in place and if they still keep coming down, put on a bandage with a pad on it, letting pad come directly over ruptured parts. Pinch, and at the same time crowd inwardly, directly over the opening, three or four times a day until healed. This irritates the lining and in a short time it will close up and be as sound as if it had never been ruptured.

HOOF OINTMENT.

Take Resin three ounces, Beeswax six ounces, Lard two pounds; melt together and pour into a pot. Add two ounces of turpentine, two ounces of finely pulrerized verdigris, one pound of tallow. Stir together until it gets cold. This is one of the best things for a horse's hoof made.

TO GROW A NEW HOOF.

The following wash will grow a new hoof onto a horse in ninety days if used according to directions: One quart of soft soap made from wood ashes, two quarts of chamber-lie, one-quarter of a pound of copperas. Put in tight can and keep well covered, stirring before using. Take a brush or swab and apply to horse's feet every morning, until they become soft. If horse is working, you can not use as freely as if not at work, as his feet will get so soft he can not travel. Anoint as high as ankles, keep feet well pared down, and shoe with shoes that will spread the foot. Shoe often, at least once a week.

TO CURE A QUARTER CRACK.

Take knife and cut crosswise of crack at top of hoof. This will start crack to running the other way and as soon as you can grow hoof out your horse is well. Use wash or hoof ointment.

CURE ALL.

Good for sore shoulder, calks, or any kind of wounds: Alcohol two ounces, water two ounces, turpentine two ounces, vinegar four ounces, two eggs. Shake well and apply to wound. You will find it a number one liniment.

FOR BARB-WIRE CUTS.

For barb-wire cuts or any old sore.—Take carbolic acid one part to twenty parts of water or a little stronger if desired.

BLISTER.

Pulverized cantharadies two drachms, powdered capsicum one drachm, spirits of turpentine two drachms, oil of organum one drachm, lard one drachm. When you blister any part of the horse rub the part you wish to blister thoroughly, and if you wish to remove any callous or enlargement shave the hair close.

BLUE MOUNTAIN SALVE.

Two oz. verdigris, 2 oz. blue vitriol, 2 oz. alum, 2 oz. resin, ½ pint turpentine, 2 lbs. of lard, 2 oz. beeswax.

LINIMENT,

For man or beast. Half oz of turpentine, 4 oz linseed oil, 2 oz aqua amonia, 2 oz origanum, 2 oz comp. tinct benzoin.

FOR INFLAMATION OF THE EYES,

Fresh wounds and Bruises. MIX.—Sugar of lead 2 oz, sulfate of zinc 21 grains, soft water one quart.

LINIMENT,

For both man and beast. MIX.—Olive oil 3 oz, cedar oil 1 oz, oil origanum 1 oz, camphor gum 1 oz, tincture cantharides 1 oz, aqua amonia 2 oz.

LAMPERS.

Prick the lampers with knife or some sharp instrument and bathe with the tincture of myrrh 1 oz, rain water 2 oz.

TO REMOVE FILM,

From the eyes of horses and cattle. Equal parts of loaf sugar, fine table salt, pulverize fine. Blow into the eye every day until cured.

ANOTHER REMEDY.—Pulverize blue vitriol one part, and loaf sugar three parts. Take a goose quill, fill it with the mixture, and blow into the eye once a day; until cured.

BOTS.

About four quarts of strong coffee will cure the bots, and is said to be good for colic.

COLD ON THE LUNGS.

Give five drops of aconite, and five drops of belladonna alternate every two hours until relieved. Give by putting on tongue. It is also good for lung fever.

FOR COLLAR GALLS.

Anoint with white lead. Another, sulphur and calomel, mix and apply as soon as collar is taken off while damp, or use cure all.

TO TAKE WARTS OFF OF HORSE.

Take a hair out of his tail and tie around the wart. It will soon cut it off. It will heal as fast as it cuts.

KIDNEY DISEASE.

Take one heaping teaspoonful of saltpetre dissolved in warm rain water, add one pint of cold after dissolving. Dose one tablespoonful every twenty four hours, repeat the dose and so on.

WHEN HORSES' BLOOD IS OUT OF ORDER.

Put a rowel in the breast, then take saltpetre, sulphur and copperas, equal parts, pulverize fine. Give two tablespoonfuls per day. Sulphur is cleansing, saltpetre cooling, and copperas is a purgative.

WHEN A HORSE IS NOT DOING WELL,

And hair looks bad, I find the following simple remedy to be very good. Give one half teacupful of black strap molasses once a day in oats.

CONDITION POWDERS.

MIX.—4 oz. finnegrate seed; 2 oz copperas, 2 oz black antimoney, 2 oz blood root pulverized, 4 oz resin, 2 oz saltpetre, 2 qts wood ashes sifted. Dose one table-spoonful once a day.

COMMON HEALING SALVE.

Take resin and beeswax, each, two ounces, sweet oil eight ounces; melt together, stirring till cold.

FOR TOOTHACHE.

Take two drams of alum in powder, and one ounce of nitrous spirits of either; mix and dissolve; apply a little to the tooth, and in the tooth if hollow.

LINIMENT FOR RHEUMATISM,

For man or beast. Four eggs, well beaten together; vinegar, one quart; spirits of turpentine, four ounces; spirits of wine, one ounce; camphor, one ounce. These ingredients to be beaten well together, then put in a bottle and shake for ten minutes after which to be corked down tightly to exclude air. In half an hour it is fit for use. To be well rubed in, two, three or four times a day, before fire.

RHEUMATISM OF LONG STANDING,

Is always chronic. When the above remedy will be useful, together with sweatning medicines. The bowels must be kept open and diet low. It is always well to keep the parts affected covered with cotton batting.

FOR RHEUMATISM.

The best external application which we have ever used is the following. I know of a case that was cured by this application of long standing. Spirits camphor one ounce; spirits of hartshorn one ounce; spirits turpentine one ounce; number six, called hot drops, one ounce; laudanum one tablespoon-ful; neats foot oil one-half pint and one beef's gall. Cut the beef's gall and let the green stuff that is in it run into a bottle, then add to it the above articles. Shake up well and cork tight; it is ready for use. The only part of the gall that is of any use is the green juice it contains. The larger the beef's gall the better. Apply three times a day, rub down freely with this liniment, and cover with cotton, as I have before told you. If you cannot use cotton rub on liniment at night and thoroughly heat it in by the fire.

GREEN SALVE.

Take resin and beeswax, each, one ounce; mutton tallow, or hog's lard about four ounces; melt altogether, and stir in one drachm of pulverized verdigris and mix well. Useful for old sores cuts, wounds, ulcers and cancers.

FOR BURNS AND SCALDS.

Common sugar house molasses is very good, if honey cannot be had. Raw potatoes scraped and mixed with sweet oil, or linseed oil. A few drops of turpentine is also a good application.

TO THROW A COW.

Take a rope tie into the halter or to horns, draw head to one side put a half hitch around back of fore legs, and another half hitch in front of hind legs, and get behind cow and pull, and cow will have to lie down.

TO MAKE THE COWS COME HOME AT NIGHT.

Make out of stiff leather a tube the shape of a length of stovepipe, of sufficient size to go on the fore leg of the bell cow and fasten it to the girt. Your cow cannot lie down to rest until the tube is off. When she comes home take it off. She soon learns to come and rest, and the rest of the cows following.

COWS WHO CAST THEIR WETHERS.

Wash wethers clean with warm milk, then bathe well with strong alum water. Sprinkle with finely powdered rosin. Run your arm in full length, hold it there until it begins to stick to your hand. Rub back with something heavy to keep them from striving while putting back the wethers. Take up hide across small of the back, put a small awl hole through the hide, and tie a string or hair around it.

TO PREVENT COW OF KICKING WHILE MILKING.

Use gag strap same as for horse, buckle tight and proceed to milk.

————[o]————

www.ingramcontent.com/pod-product-compliance
Lightning Source LLC
Chambersburg PA
CBHW031747090426
42739CB00008B/913